THE HIGHWAY COMPANION

THE HIGHWAY COMPANION

HARRY SECOMBE

Robson Books

Designed by Harold King

Researched by Angela Pollard

First published in Great Britain in 1987 by Robson Books Ltd, Bolsover House, 5–6 Clipstone Street, London W1P 7EB.

Copyright © 1987 Harry Secombe; copyright of individual items listed on p. 144.

British Library Cataloguing in Publication Data

Secombe, Harry
  The Highway companion: inspirational words along the way.
  1. Devotional literature
  I. Title
  242   BV4832.2
  ISBN 0-86051-430-7

Printed in Great Britain by
St Edmundsbury Press Ltd, Bury St Edmunds, Suffolk
Bound by Dorstel Press Ltd, Harlow, Essex

The Generations

Home and Away

Be Of Good Comfort

CONTENTS

The Poet's Voice

Say A Little Prayer

FOREWORD

Whenever anyone in my profession tells me he is doing a one-man show I have to smile, because there is no such thing. There have to be other people involved behind the scenes: the stage manager and his team, the lighting man, the box-office staff, etc etc...

The same principle applies to 'Highway'. I present the show in front of the camera but there are great numbers of people out of sight of the lens who do at least as much as I do in the making of the programme.

Let's start with the Central Unit, the staff who co-ordinate all 'Highway' productions. There is Bill Ward, the Executive Producer, a man with fifty years of television experience who persuaded me to do it in the first place and is responsible for scheduling all the programmes. Then there is Ronnie Cass, who makes sure that what I have to say on 'Highway' makes sense, who arranges the many music sessions, who writes many of the songs I sing, who also accompanies me on the piano, and who has done the lion's share in producing this book. Angela Pollard, whose official title is Programme Co-ordinator, keeps everybody on the right track. She is a wonderful administrator and this book, which she has painstakingly researched, was her idea.

We four are just the tip of the iceberg. No fewer than eleven different regional TV companies share in producing 'Highway'. That means eleven different producers and directors with their personal assistants, researchers and camera crews. Add to all those people the guest artists, musicians and interviewees and the number runs well into the hundreds.

So if anything ever should go wrong on 'Highway', it's not all my fault!

H.S.

INTRODUCTION

Towards the end of 1986 I celebrated my first forty years in show-business, and I realised with a start that almost ten per cent of that time had been spent on one programme, 'Highway'.

At a time when I was beginning to think I had done just about everything that a varied career had to offer, 'Highway' came along to turn that theory on its head.

Let me try and expand on that to explain what I mean. 'Highway' was the first programme in which I had become involved, where the divide of a 'theatre curtain' could be removed. In it, I find that I am talking - and listening - to people face to face, up and down this wonderful land of ours. Working on 'Highway' has made me feel very humble. Until I became involved in it, I had no idea how many thousands - yes thousands - of people devote their lives unselfishly, without thought of reward, to helping others less fortunate than themselves.

And as I became aware of this, so I've found growing a pride in the series - I've discovered,

little by little, that people were not merely enjoying 'Highway', they were being comforted by it. Please don't think that I am immodestly claiming the credit for myself – I'm too long in the tooth to be that self-deceptive. Just being a part is reward enough for me. No, the comfort and inspiration people derive from 'Highway' can be ascribed to two things.

The first is the people who have appeared on it. We've been fortunate enough to meet the incredible Evelyn Glennie, the profoundly deaf percussion player who in the comparatively short life of 'Highway' has attended the Royal Academy of Music, won the Shell Young Percussionist of the Year award, given solo concerts in the Wigmore Hall, and has now joined the 'Highway' Orchestra as their regular percussionist.

Then there's been Dr Peter Griffiths, who threw up a lucrative practice in South London to found and maintain a hospice in Tŷ Olwen near Swansea, and who hopes to open another one soon in Llanelli.

And Carolyn James, who became blind a few years ago, and who has since that time become a water colour artist of some renown, with many exhibitions to her credit. Carolyn has also developed her talent as a lyric writer and has had her songs performed by Dana and by Ian Wallace as well as by myself.

And Cantor Ernest Levy of Glasgow: a man who teaches the true meaning of tolerance, having emerged from the war after being in eleven concentration camps (twice in Belsen) without the slightest trace of bitterness.

And Dr Lloyd, who runs the premature baby unit in Aberdeen; and Mrs Cole of Gloucester who inspired by showing how her faith helped her overcome her multiple sclerosis; and the radiant Laura Morris of Caerphilly who, since conquering lymph cancer six years ago, has become an air hostess, but devotes every minute of her spare time raising money for the hospital which helped to cure her.

I could go on, but I think I've made the point. Let me get on to the second source of inspiration and comfort that 'Highway' provides: it is the weekly reading.

I'm flattered at the letters I receive from you all, telling me what you'd like me to sing, but we receive many, many more requests at the 'Highway' office asking for copies of last Sunday's reading. When Bernard Cribbins read 'Death is Nothing at All', we had to admit defeat. There was no way we could cope with the demand. So we did the only thing possible, we printed the reading in the *TV Times*. The thousands of letters we have received have not merely occasioned a reply. What they have done is persuaded us that it would be a good idea to

make a selection of the most inspiring readings from all the 'Highway' programmes so far, and to gather them together for a book.

Who made this selection, you might ask? The answer is simple. You did. You did it by your letters. I have tried to help by filling in the odd detail of who read what and when.

I do hope that you will enjoy this book, which has been compiled for you with love. If it also brings you comfort that will be an added bonus.

HARRY SECOMBE

The Generations

While we were in Norwich I visited a retirement home, which must surely be one of the loveliest and best-planned not merely in Britain but in the world. The homes and gardens of Norwich's Great Hospital are thoughtfully laid out in a setting which is itself idyllic and peaceful. A sign on the wall sums up the optimistic mood of the residents.

WE WILL NOT WEEP

We will not weep that Spring be passed
and Autumn shadows fall.
These years shall be, although advanced,
the loveliest of all.

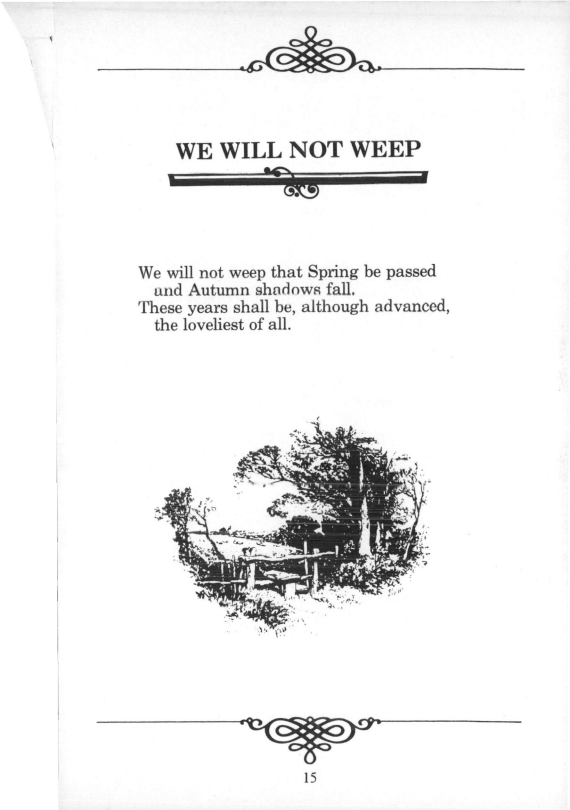

I've always been attracted by the lines from the song 'Kids' which go: 'Why can't they be like we were. Perfect in every way. What's the matter with kids today?'

Well, speaking personally – in the words of Paul Daniels – not a lot.

But, like every mature parent, I have felt – four times in my case – that sinking feeling as you realise a child has become an adult. Cecil Day Lewis wrote a poem about it that described it perfectly, and sums it up in one magic line: 'Love is proved in the letting go'. It was read for us by the Reverend Neville Boundy in our Bristol programme.

Parents: read and recognise. Parents-to-be: read and get an insight into the future.

WALKING AWAY

For Sean

It is eighteen years ago, almost to the day,
A sunny day with the leaves just turning,
The touch-lines new ruled, since I watched you
    play
Your first game of football, then, like a satellite
Wrenched from its orbit, go drifting away.

Behind a scatter of boys, I can see
You walking away from me towards the school,
With the pathos of a half-fledged thing set free
Into a wilderness, the gait of one
Who finds no path where the path should be.

That hesitant figure, eddying away
Like a winged seed loosened from its parent stem
Has something I never quite grasp to convey
About Nature's give-and-take, the small, the
    scorching
Ordeals which fire one's irresolute clay.

I have had worse partings, but none that so
Gnaws at my mind still. Perhaps it is roughly
Saying what God alone could perfectly show,
How selfhood begins with a walking away,
And love is proved in the letting go.

C. Day Lewis (1904-72)

17

I think it was Oscar Wilde who wrote that 'Of all forms of sympathy, sympathy with suffering is the least fine mode. It contains in it some of our own terror.'

I suppose it's a latent fear that makes us turn away from what we see as suffering when we are not personally involved. Understandable, possibly, but it can lead to assumptions as impertinent as they are fallacious.

Consider the obvious joy the next poem tells of. The parents of Ruth knew that their daughter, who was educationally sub-normal, would die in her twenties. But the life of this 'handicapped' child gave her parents much. The Reverend Amos Cresswell read the poem, called simply 'Ruth', during our visit to Exeter.

RUTH

Ruth is in the garden to be found,
For it is only there that she can find,
Such ample, blissful pleasures to abound,
And captivate her simple childish mind.

For there are rounded pebbles on the drive,
And coloured petals standing row on row,
With aeroplanes above that zoom and dive,
Though what they mean to her we'll never know.

There she can run unchecked with all her might,
Chase the capricious wind without a care,
Pause by the kitchen window for a sight,
So reassuring, of her mother there.

Such tiny pleasures fill her numbered hours,
So when she comes to meet Thee, Lord, we pray,
That she may find a garden such as ours,
And someone there to watch her at her play.

Irvonwy Morgan (1907-82)

*A*re you sitting comfortably? Then I'll begin.' Unmistakable words known to millions, words associated of course with Julia Lang from the days when she introduced 'Listen with Mother', and children and mothers all over the country sat down at a quarter to two to listen to the radio for fifteen minutes.

We had the most wonderful talk down in Suffolk, and Julia naturally chose a reading on the subject of the young. It is derived from St Mark's Gospel, Chapter 10, and was written in 1950 by a French monk, the Abbé Michel Quoist, author of many books of prayers and meditations.

OF SUCH IS THE KINGDOM
OF GOD

God says: I like youngsters. I want people to be like them.

I don't like old people unless they are still children. I want only children in my kingdom; this has been decreed from the beginning of time.

Youngsters — twisted, humped, wrinkled, white-bearded — all kinds of youngsters, but youngsters.

There is no changing it, it has been decided, there is room for no one else.

I like little children because my likeness has not yet been dulled in them.

They have not botched my likeness, they are new, pure, without a blot, without a smear.

So, when I gently lean over them, I recognise myself in them. I like them because they are still growing, they are still improving.

They are on the road, they are on their way. But with grown-ups there is nothing to expect any more.

They will no longer grow, no longer improve.
They have come to a full stop...

Alleluia! Alleluia! Open, all of you, little old men!
It is I, your God, the Eternal, risen from the dead,
coming to bring back to life the child in you.

Hurry! Now is the time. I am ready to give you
again the beautiful face of a child, the beautiful
eyes of a child...

For I love youngsters, and I want everyone to
be like them.

Michel Quoist

When 'Highway' visited Jersey, we went to a remarkable school called Bel Royal in which normal and handicapped children receive their education side by side. This was due in large measure to the Head-teacher, Mrs Wendy Hurford, who refused to accept the idea that disabled children should be kept in a special unit. One of the handicapped children there was Angus Rymer and he delivered his own poem, which he wrote when he was 10, on the subject of friendship with all the technique of a skilled actor.

WITHOUT A FRIEND

To have no friends is a terrible thing
Left out of simply everything
No games, no fun, no sweets to share
Driven so mad that you despair
Bullied, mocked and kicked about
Driven so mad and you want to shout
   and scream and kick and hit about
Until you feel so ill you hurt
To have no friends is a terrible thing
Left out of simply everything

Angus Rymer

When 'Highway' went to Peterborough I met a Jewish couple, Harry and Lotte Kramer, who told me about their childhood together in Mainz. How they were separated when the Nazi oppression began, then met again in England after the war and married.

Lotte had found it difficult in the past to talk about what happened to her family at the outbreak of war and in the concentration camps, but she finally found an outlet in her poetry. She remembered her grandfather's death vividly. He was a butcher in their village, and he died of a heart attack when he found his shop barricaded by Nazi storm-troopers who were making people boycott Jewish shops.

He may have been killed by the Nazis but he lives on graphically in Lotte Kramer's poem, which was read by Penny Little.

GRANDFATHER

For me
He was the unassailable giant
The creator of bicycles and dolls,
The law of God behind his butcher's apron.

He smelt
Of sausages and fresh air,
And he grew out of his small town
As naturally as a Black Forest pine tree.

Not quite
In tune he would sing to me
With tears in his voice and eyes,
His well-worn folk-songs and ballads

His word
Was gospel to his family,
And his wife's large domesticity
Was ornament and shape for his great size.

No one
Dared to correct him.
For him it was right to stub his roll
To saturate his moustache and napkin,

So when one April Fool's Day
They barricaded his shop and house,
He, like an angry god, turned away
   from the living.

Lotte Kramer

This next poem was written by Mrs Ann Standen of Bury St Edmunds, and sent in by her fourteen-year-old daughter Alison, who felt it would 'help lots of other people who have just had a handicapped baby and are frightened about what the future will hold.' Though it hasn't yet been read on 'Highway', I wanted to include it in this book because of the message it offers.

'Our Little Fella' also has a message for the rest of us: Mrs Standen wrote it to tell those who rudely turn to stare at Martin that he is her son, and she loves him - as do her husband, and their three other children. This little boy is part of their family, and belongs in the warmth of their family circle: imagine how painful they find the reactions of those thoughtless people who gawp, or even say things such as, 'Children like that should be put away!' We, too, must learn to love 'God's gift of a child'.

OUR LITTLE FELLA

'A precious gift of a son', we read
In our Press's column of birth.
You do not know, you folks out there,
It's not always an occasion of mirth.

'Your son is a mongol,' the Doctor's voice said –
His eyes were kindly and hurt.
Our hearts missed a beat, our eyes brimmed
  with tears;
'It's not true,' said our minds, filled with
  unspoken fears.

Nobody told us upon that sad day
What a joy a mongol can be.
We only knew, as they left us alone,
He could die by the time he was three.

But God gave us that child
And the strength to go on and survive;
He knew in His wisdom how Martin could be –
God spared him, and now he is five.

There are black days, and sad days
When the man on the street stops to stare,
Do you know, folks out there, as your eyes turn
   and glare –
You are looking at God's special care.

He is so full of fun, and energy too,
He gives love wherever he goes;
And he's so filled with trust in each person he
   meets
From the top of his head to his toes.

So if you hear these words
At the birth of your child
And the bottom drops out of your world:
Your heart will not break
If with love you will take
That step out, and remember within:
That babe you have borne is still God's gift of a
   child.

Ann Standen

ere's a song that keeps one generation in touch with another; it was written by Jimmy Grafton – my manager for many years, a great friend and an even better writer – and it tells you all you need to know about him. A writer should be remembered by his words – so let it be with Jimmy. (The music for 'When You Look Back On Your Life' was written by Cyril Ornadel, who also wrote that for the song which has almost become my signature tune: 'If I Ruled the World'.)

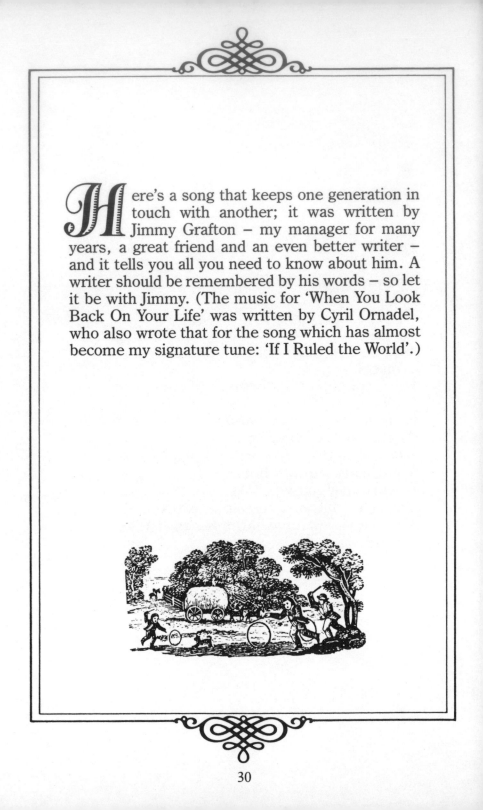

WHEN YOU LOOK BACK ON YOUR LIFE

When you look back on your life,
What will you see?
Will you see the kind of man
You want to be?
Will you know, deep in your heart,
In all you've tried
You've worked with dignity,
With passion, and with pride?

When you look back on your life,
What will you say
To companions who were with you on the way?
Will you hold your head up high before the rest
Because you know you've done your best?

On the voyage through life
Some seas are rough;
There will be times your best will not seem quite
    enough.
Then you must ride the storm
Just hanging on,
And when the calm has come again,
You'll still go on.

When you look back on your life,
What will you find
That has given you the greatest
Peace of mind?
When all is said and done,
Let it not be what you've won, my son,
But that you lived your life with love.

Jimmy Grafton

People vary so much in their attitude towards growing old; some people seem to worry about it so much they don't enjoy themselves while they're not old! Well, I've been growing older ever since the day I was born, and so far I've never been bothered. Quite the contrary. A few years ago, a good friend, Ben Nisbet, wrote a song for me on the subject.

It was a song that applied especially to me, but anybody can take encouragement from the theme of the song, which says very simply:

> *And yet*
> *It seems to me*
> *The best is yet to be*

AND YET

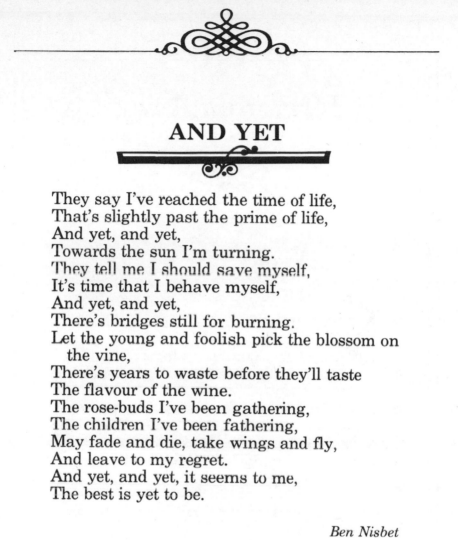

They say I've reached the time of life,
That's slightly past the prime of life,
And yet, and yet,
Towards the sun I'm turning.
They tell me I should save myself,
It's time that I behave myself,
And yet, and yet,
There's bridges still for burning.
Let the young and foolish pick the blossom on
   the vine,
There's years to waste before they'll taste
The flavour of the wine.
The rose-buds I've been gathering,
The children I've been fathering,
May fade and die, take wings and fly,
And leave to my regret.
And yet, and yet, it seems to me,
The best is yet to be.

Ben Nisbet

Home and Away

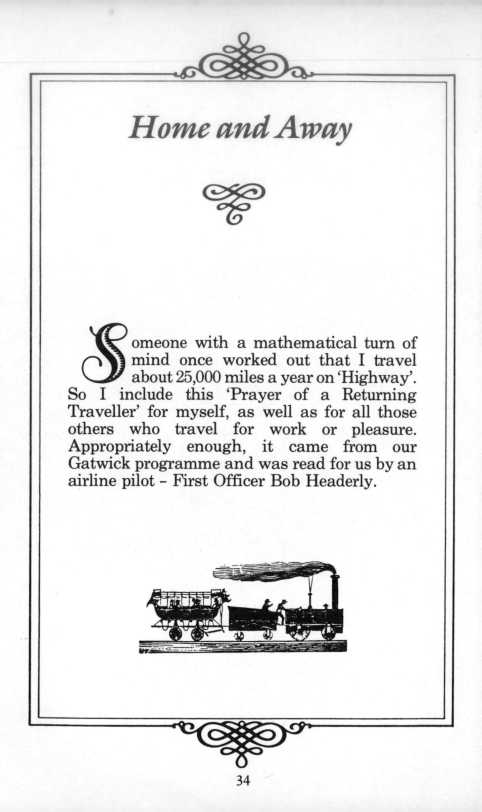

Someone with a mathematical turn of mind once worked out that I travel about 25,000 miles a year on 'Highway'. So I include this 'Prayer of a Returning Traveller' for myself, as well as for all those others who travel for work or pleasure. Appropriately enough, it came from our Gatwick programme and was read for us by an airline pilot – First Officer Bob Headerly.

PRAYER OF A RETURNING
TRAVELLER

Blessed are you, Lord God,
King of all creation,
You have made this beautiful
  world for our pleasure.
We praise you that we have seen
  its wonders;
  its mountains and forests,
  its rivers, lakes and seas.

We praise you that you have given
  your people
Agile minds and skilful hands
  to use this world's resources well.

We thank you that in every nation
  we find people like ourselves
  who know your name and serve you.

Thank you for bringing us home in
  safety.
Thank you for the family and friends
  we return to.
Keep us always in your love, O Lord
  our God.

All praise and glory is yours, Father
Through Jesus Christ your Son,
  in the love of the Holy Spirit,
  God for ever and ever.   *Amen*

*H*ere's a story that could only have happened on 'Highway'. A viewer sent us a song lyric with two conditions attached: she was to remain anonymous, and anything her words earned was to go to the Musicians' Union Benevolent Fund, to repay the pleasure musicians had brought to her life. We observed her conditions and used her beautiful song – which has become a viewers' favourite.

COVER ME WITH LOVE

Cover me with roses, wet with morning dew;
Cover me with starshine, and sweet rainbows'
    hue.
Cover me with soft leaves on an Autumn day,
Cover me with happiness as I go on my way.

Cover me with raindrops when my heart is dry;
Cover me with snowflakes from an icy blue
    sky.
Cover me with kisses, when as friends we meet –
Cover me with love, dear Lord, as I listen at Thy
    feet.

And when my journey's over, and I've ceased to
    be,
Cover me with peace, dear Lord, as I journey
    back to Thee.

On one of my trips to Scotland I went to Blantyre and the David Livingstone Centre and there I met Edna Healey (wife of the Labour Party politician, Denis Healey). She was making a film and writing a book about Mary Moffat, who in 1844 married the great Scots missionary and explorer, thus adding weight to the saying 'behind every great man, there's a great woman'.

This lovely poem by Mary not only tells how she was missing her explorer husband, but also shows how her love remains undimmed by his absence. Mary died in 1862, eleven years before her husband.

In my business I've been on the road quite a lot, sometimes for months on end, but I've never had such a poem written for me by my wife Myra!

A HUNDRED THOUSAND WELCOMES

A hundred thousand welcomes
And it's time for you to come
From the far land of the foreigner
To your country and your home.
Do you think I would reproach you
With the sorrows that I bore?
Since the sorrow is all over now
I have you here once more.

You'll never part me, darling,
There's a promise in your eye;
I may tend you while I'm living,
You will watch me when I die.
And if death but kindly lead me
To the blessed home on high,
What a hundred thousand welcomes
Will await you in the sky.

Mary Livingstone (1821-62)

*H*aving visited so many towns and cities in the last four years, some of them tend to become a little blurred in my mind. But one town remains crystal clear, thanks to John Arlott. John was of course the doyen of radio cricket commentators, giving us his word pictures so vivid you actually felt you were witnessing the action being described.

But as a poet John is equally graphic – I know of no poem that evokes a town as clearly as 'Southampton' does. John read the poem for us himself, in that unmistakable sonorous voice. From Southampton of course – where else?

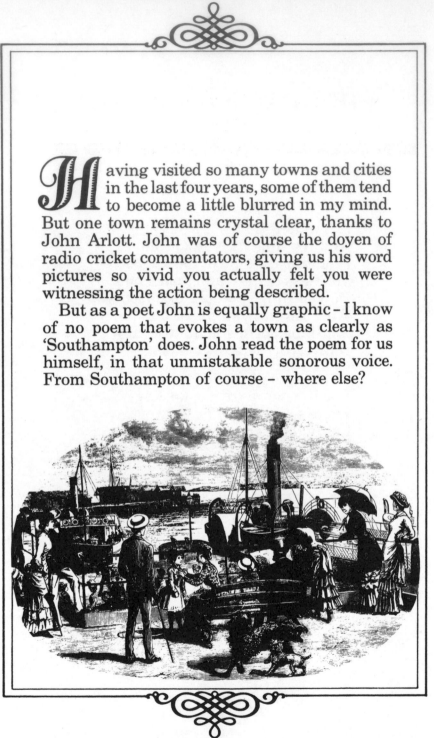

SOUTHAMPTON

The ocean liners' towering funnels
Looming over the gaunt, bent cranes
Merge with the town like painted turrets
Springing from the dock-side lanes.

Galleon tram-cars gong and rattle
Round the Bargate to the Quay
And the unexpected glimpses
Of a grey, unsea-like sea.

On the wharves each blear-eyed warehouse
Blunts the tang of sailors' tales:
Strictly business: care with cargoes:
Scour the cabins: stow the mails.

Come cruising from 'The Ocean's Gateway'.
Will you go White Star or Red?
Dancing, cocktails, Tourist Class,
Put to sea on a feather-bed.

There are elms along The Avenue
Where General Gordon rode,
And milk-bottles daily broken
On Honeysuckle Road.

John Arlott (b. 1914)

There has been a tendency over the years to devalue the currency of patriotism. Such sayings as 'Patriotism is the last refuge of a scoundrel' have contributed to this. But for the life of me I can see no wrong in loving our own country. Certainly my travels in 'Highway' have helped to reinforce my love for the British Isles.

This poem, 'Invocation', by William Browne which was read for us by Sir Michael Hordern at Tavistock, says it all.

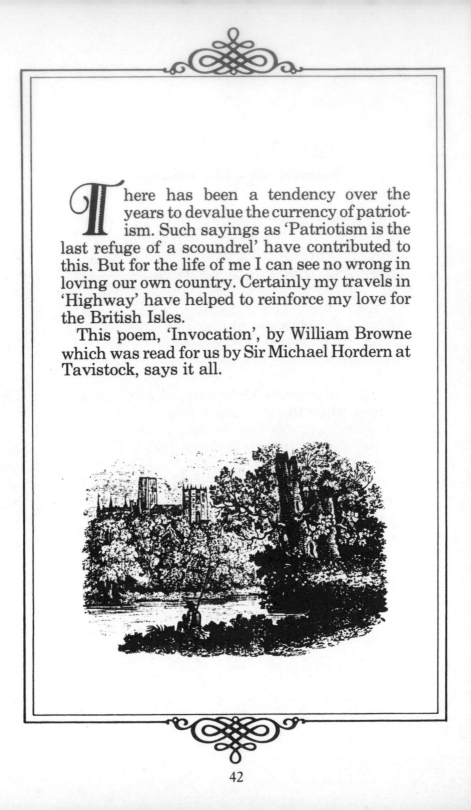

INVOCATION

Hail, thou my native soil! Thou blessed plot
Whose equal all the world affordeth not!
Show me who can so many crystal rills,
Such sweet-cloth'd valleys or aspiring hills
Such wood-ground, pastures, quarries, wealthy
   mines;
Such rocks in whom the diamond fairly shines
And if the earth can show the like again,
Yet will she fail in her sea-ruling men.
Time never can produce men to o'ertake
The fames of Grenville, Davis, Gilbert, Drake
Or worthy Hawkins, or of thousands more
That by their power made the Devonian shore
Mock the proud Tagus; for whose richest spoil
The boasting Spaniard left the Indian soil
Bankrupt of store, knowing it would quit cost
By winning this, though all the rest were lost.

William Browne (1590-1645)

We live in a high-tech world which is becoming more and more complicated. Being a man who has but lately mastered the intricacies of electricity (you work it by putting on the switch), I am fast falling behind in my attempts to master modern-day miracles. But when you get down to it – what are we all searching for?

The following piece is part of a longer poem, *The Wish*, written by Abraham Cowley over three hundred years ago, and yet I venture to believe that his stated ambitions vary very little from most of ours. Have a read and see what you think.

The poem was read for us by comedy actor Jack Smethurst on our Lynton programme.

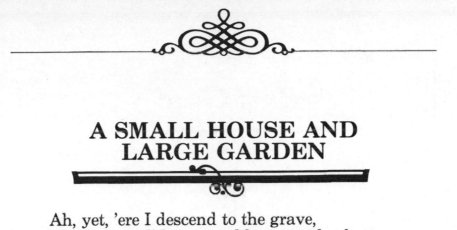

A SMALL HOUSE AND LARGE GARDEN

Ah, yet, 'ere I descend to the grave,
May I a small house and large garden have;
And a few friends, and many books, both true,
Both wise, and both delightful too!
And since love ne'er will from me flee,
A mistress moderately fair,
And good as guardian angels are,
Only beloved and loving me.

O fountains! when in you shall I
Myself eased of unpeaceful thoughts espy?
O fields! O woods! when, when shall I be made
The happy tenant of your shade?
Here's the spring-head of Pleasure's flood;
Here's wealthy Nature's treasury,
Where all the riches lie that she
Has coin'd and stamp'd for good.

Abraham Cowley (1618-67)

Be of Good Comfort

When 'Highway' went to Middlesbrough, Anna Raeburn – who began her stage career in the Little Theatre there – read an excerpt from Anne Frank's *The Diary of a Young Girl*. Born in 1929, Anne spent her early teens (1942-44) hiding from the Nazis in an office building in Amsterdam, and she has left a record of her thoughts and experiences in the diary she kept. (She was among the thousands who died in the Nazi concentration camp at Belsen.)

If anything better has ever been written to illustrate the unconquerable human spirit I have yet to read it. Nor will I forget the way every member of the crew was affected, both by Anne Frank's words and Anna Raeburn's moving reading.

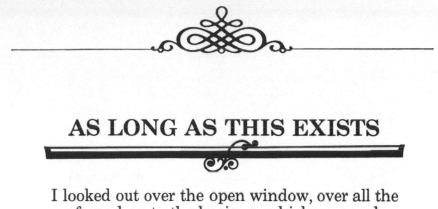

AS LONG AS THIS EXISTS

I looked out over the open window, over all the roofs and on to the horizon, which was such a pale blue that it was hard to see the dividing line.

'As long as this exists,' I thought, 'and I may live to see it, this sunshine, the cloudless skies, while this lasts, I cannot be unhappy.'

The best remedy for those who are afraid, lonely or unhappy is to go outside, somewhere they can be quiet, alone with the heavens, nature and God. Because only then does one feel that all is as it should be and that God wishes to see people happy, amidst the simple beauty of nature. As long as this exists, and it certainly always will, I know that then there will be comfort for every sorrow, whatever the circumstances may be. And I firmly believe that nature brings solace in all troubles.

O who knows, perhaps it won't be long before I can share this overwhelming feeling of bliss with someone who feels the way I do about it. Yours, Anne.

Anne Frank (1929-45)

My mother used to tell me, 'If you give to ten beggars and nine are fakes, it's worth it for the one who is genuine.'

I wonder if she realised she was passing on the message given in the Gospel according to Matthew, chapter 25, verses 31 to 40. This passage was read by Father Ambrose during our first programme from Glasgow.

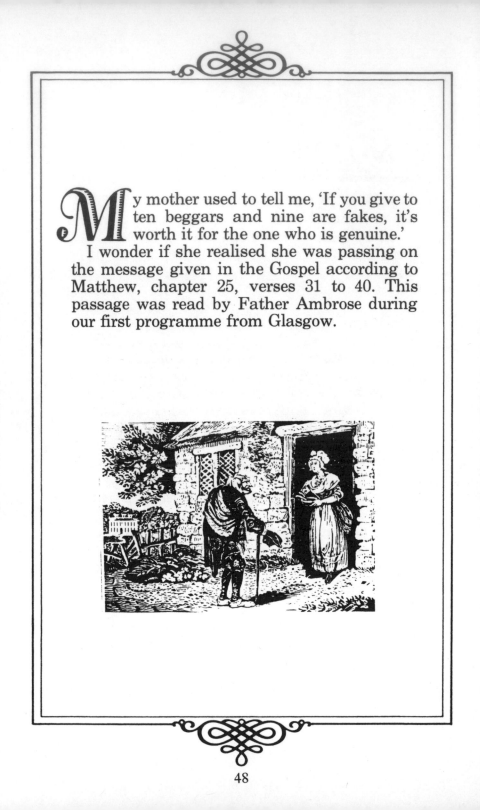

THE FINAL JUDGEMENT

When the Son of Man comes as King and all the angels with him, he will sit on his royal throne, and the people of all the nations will be gathered before him. Then he will divide them into two groups, just as a shepherd separates the sheep from the goats. He will put the righteous people on his right and the others on his left. Then the King will say to the people on his right, 'Come, you that are blessed by my Father! Come and possess the kingdom which has been prepared for you ever since the creation of the world. I was hungry and you fed me, thirsty and you gave me a drink; I was a stranger and you received me in your homes, naked and you clothed me; I was sick and you took care of me, in prison and you visited me.'

The righteous will then answer him, 'When, Lord, did we ever see you hungry and feed you, or thirsty and give you a drink? When did we ever see you a stranger and welcome you in our homes, or naked and clothe you? When did we ever see you sick or in prison, and visit you?' The King will reply, 'I tell you, whenever you did this for one of the least important of these brothers of mine, you did it for me!'

Matthew 25: 31-40

We inscribe the names of those dear to us on their tombstones, together with brief details of their lives – the dates of birth and death, perhaps a word or two about their occupation – and that's enough for their family and friends to remember them by.

But occasionally we find an epitaph which goes a great deal further than this, and Arthur Marshall has long taken a delight in visiting graveyards and cemeteries to 'collect' unusual inscriptions. In our programme from Exeter he read what must be the star of his collection. We don't know who wrote this watchmaker's epitaph; it seems possible to me that George Routleigh might even have done it himself.

A WATCHMAKER'S EPITAPH

Here lies in horizontal position
The outside case of
George Routleigh, Watchmaker,
Whose abilities in that line were an honour
To his profession:
Integrity was the main-spring
and Prudence the regulator
Of all the actions of his life:
Humane, generous, and liberal,
His hand never stopped
Till he had relieved distress;
So nicely regulated were all his movements
That he never went wrong
Except when set a-going
By people who did not know his key:
Even then, he was easily set right again:
He had the art of disposing of his time
So well, that his hours glided away
In one continual round of Pleasure and Delight,

Till an unlucky moment put a period to
His existence;
He departed this life November 14, 1802
  Aged 57,
Wound up in hope of being taken in hand by his
  maker
And of being
Thoroughly cleaned, repaired and set a-going
In the World to come.

Epitaph at Lydford

*I*t was a moving occasion when 'Highway' visited Stoke Mandeville, and our reading that week was particulary poignant. It was written as well as delivered by Norman Tebbit as his personal tribute to the work of that wonderful hospital. But it went far beyond that, because it demonstrated how faith can be enhanced through suffering. Norman Tebbit's personal involvement with the hospital through the tragic paralysis of his wife, as a result of the bombing of the Grand Hotel in Brighton, is of course well known.

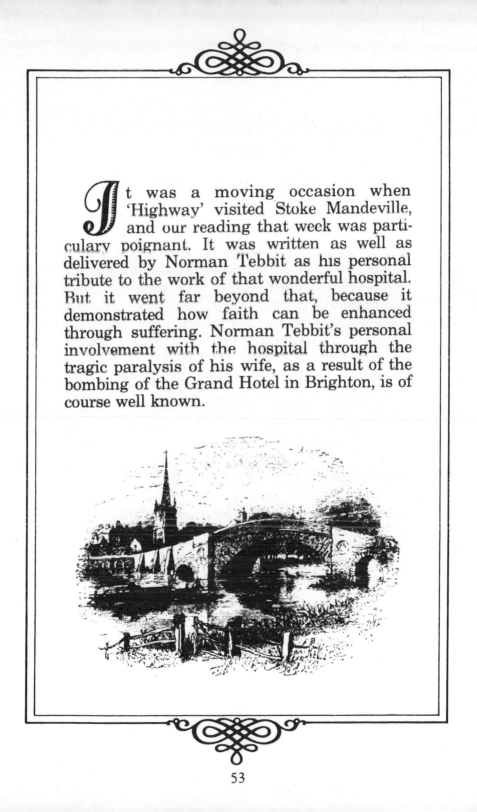

SOMETHING GOOD CAN EMERGE

It is easy in my profession to become cynical about people. A while here in Stoke Mandeville can bring you a different view. People come here with terrible injuries, frightened and in pain. Some recover fully. For them that sickening moment on the sports field, in the wreckage of a car, or at the foot of the stairs, that sickening moment of realisation that their limbs no longer work, will fade to just a memory. Others will learn to live a near-normal life, though unable to run or walk. Others will live in an unending battle against pain and a constant struggle to retain dignity and purpose without use of legs or hands and arms or even speech itself.

Believe me – there is nothing ennobling or spiritual about a shattered spine or the suffering it brings to the victim and his or her family and friends. Yet somehow, from beyond that pain and suffering, something good can emerge. As we bemoan our lot, an attack of flu, a late train, a family quarrel or some material want, we may lose sight of more important things. In our

imperfect world we may even lose sight of the human spirit which is fundamentally good. That spirit is certainly to be found here in the victims, their families and friends.

You will not merely see tears but hear laughter on the wards. No more than tears can laughter wash away tragedy and suffering, but it marks the spirit by which they are overcome. And there is a strength which flows from the sharing between patients and between families of the pain of suffering, and the joy of recovery, for here we know we each need, and we each can give, support to the others. For many that support springs also from their belief in God – a belief and trust that survives the question: 'What have I done to deserve this?'

For some it is here that, by turning to God for the first time, he is found. I hope you will never be brought here as a victim nor sit at the bedside of a loved one. Either is to know tragedy and suffering. But should that be, you will find something that perhaps you did not know – something strong and good that you may call courage, or love, or strength, or God.

Norman Tebbit (b. 1931)

I've always been curious to know which doctor my doctor goes to see when *he* is ill. That doctor must be pretty good, I reckon. In a similar way I'm interested to find out what people who are in the public eye, and sometimes expected to dispense wisdom to others, find helps them through life. It was a question I asked Jilly Cooper when I spoke to her in Stroud.

She told me she found her spiritual guidance in the following passage. 'It sums up everything for me,' she said, 'and I recommend everybody to read it each morning to get them through the day.'

I SHALL NOT PASS THIS
WAY AGAIN

I expect to pass through this world but once.
Any good thing therefore that I can do, or
   any kindness that
I can show to any fellow creature,
Let me do it now.
Let me not defer or neglect it.
For I shall not pass this way again.

Stephen Grellet (1773-1855)

Without doubt, the most popular reading ever on 'Highway' was 'Death is Nothing at All'. It was read most movingly by Bernard Cribbins on the Remembrance Day programme which came from the beaches of Normandy in November 1985.

It's funny how these things occur. We were putting the Remembrance Day programme together, and looking for a suitable reading when a 'Highway' viewer solved the problem for us.

Mr L.A. Maxim of Sudbury in Suffolk wrote to us, saying that his wife had loved these words, written by a Canon Henry Scott Holland (1847-1918), and that they had been read by the rector at her funeral service three years previously. He hoped they might bring comfort to others. We owe Mr Maxim grateful thanks for bringing them to our attention, so that we could share them with our audience.

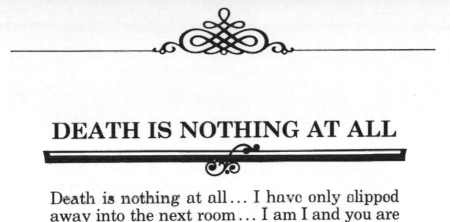

DEATH IS NOTHING AT ALL

Death is nothing at all... I have only slipped away into the next room... I am I and you are you... whatever we were to each other, that we are still. Call me by my old familiar name, speak to me in the easy way which you always used. Put no difference into your tone, wear no forced air of solemnity or sorrow. Laugh as we always laughed at the little jokes we enjoyed together. Play, smile, think of me, pray for me.

Let my name be ever the household word that it always was. Let it be spoken without effect, without the ghost of a shadow on it. Life means all that it ever meant. It is the same as it ever was, there is absolutely unbroken continuity. What is this death but a negligible accident? Why should I be out of mind because I am out of sight? I am just waiting for you, for an interval, somewhere very near, just around the corner... All is well.

Canon Henry Scott Holland

*H*ere is one of my favourite prayers, 'Everything I Had Hoped For'. It was read by Ian McIlhenny in our programme from Strabane, and is attributed to a Confederate soldier during the American Civil War. It teaches a great lesson, that your prayers will be answered, but maybe not in the way you expect.

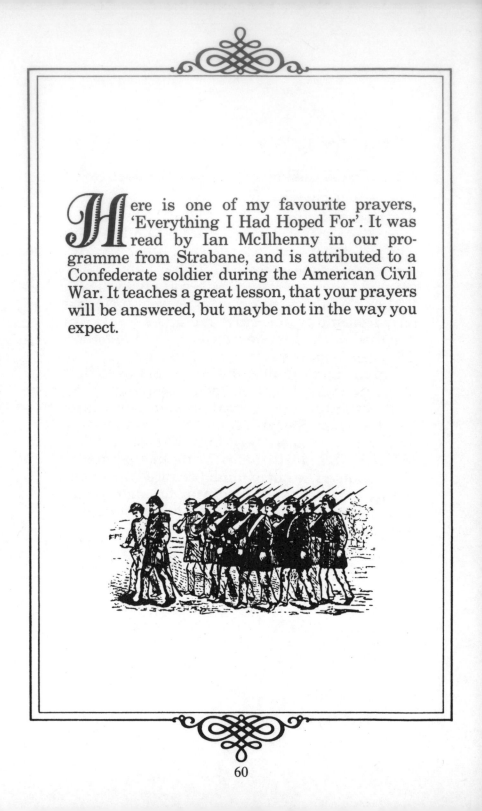

EVERYTHING I HAD HOPED FOR

I asked God for strength, that I might achieve;
   I was made weak, that I might learn humbly
   to obey,
I asked for health, that I might do greater
   things; I was given infirmity, that I might do
   better things,
I asked for riches, that I might be happy; I was
   given poverty, that I might be wise,
I asked for power, that I might have the praise of
   men; I was given weakness, that I might feel
   the need of God.
I asked for all things, that I might enjoy life; I
   was given life, that I might enjoy all things,
I got nothing that I asked for - but everything
   I had hoped for.
Almost despite myself, my unspoken prayers
   were answered,
I am, among all men, most richly blessed.

Unknown Confederate soldier

*F*ather Andrew McMahon is a Franciscan who devotes his life to the Society of St Dismas, a home for down-and-outs in Southampton. His words on 'Highway', and our visit to St Dismas, affected viewers so much, that for days, weeks and months afterwards St Dismas was inundated with gifts of money and clothing.

Father McMahon's message was as forthright as you would expect from such an uncompromising man. Uncompromising, I would add hastily, in his determination to devote himself tirelessly in his chosen task – to help his fellow man.

ON BEING POOR

I feel that, in the world we're living in today, what's needed very often is someone to articulate the problems of people who are poor. That's the Franciscan message for today: to try to get other people to understand the dilemma of being poor in our society, the dilemma of being homeless, the dilemma of just making yourself understood. Now if St Dismas is about that, I think it's about the message of St Francis, and I think it's also about the message of Christianity.

I think a man's humanity is what his spirituality is about. If people are trying to be fully human and to develop that humanity in peace and in justice and in fraternity and in service – those are all spiritual things to me. Someone once said you shouldn't talk about the Holy Communion to someone who's got an empty belly: let him find out what food is about and then talk about Holy Communion. That's the kind of thing I think the workers at St Dismas believe in.

Father Andrew McMahon

ontrast these two sayings. The first I attribute to my father. 'God doesn't think much of money,' he used to tell me. 'Look at the people he gives it to.'

The second is credited to Sam Goldwyn. 'The man who said money isn't everything is still seeing his psychiatrist.'

Neither remark is quite true of course, but this short sermon read by Father Dennis Finbow in our Peterborough programme, and based on chapter 19, verse 24, of St Matthew's Gospel, points out clearly that money in itself is neither good nor evil. It all comes down to the use we make of it.

SALVATION THROUGH
WEALTH

The Saviour says: 'Woe to the rich; it is easier for a camel to pass through the eye of a needle than for a rich man to be saved.' But those who use their riches well, who use them to clothe the naked, to feed the poor hungry people, to give drink to the thirsty, to take in the traveller, they who without vainglory and without ambition give their superfluous goods to the poor, they, I say, have a means of salvation in their wealth, and know how to change their riches, which are truly thorns, into flowers for eternity. Believe me: when God gives wealth to a man, he gives him a grace, but this grace is greater when he inspires him with the courage to put that wealth to good use.

Father Dennis Finbow

*I*n the very first series of 'Highway' we went to Durham for our Remembrance Day programme, and one of my guests was Wendy Craig.

For anyone who has suffered the pangs of separation, the poem she read by Christina Rossetti will stir poignant emotions. It would have been difficult to have chosen a reading more appropriate for the occasion.

REMEMBER

Remember me when I am gone away,
Gone far away into the silent land;
When you can no more hold me by the hand,
Nor I half turn to go yet turning stay.
Remember me when no more day by day
You tell me of our future that you planned:
Only remember me; you understand
It will be late to counsel then or pray.
Yet if you should forget me for a while
And afterwards remember, do not grieve;
For if the darkness and corruption leave
A vestige of the thoughts that once I had,
Better by far you should forget and smile
Than that you should remember and be sad.

Christina Rossetti (1830-91)

'Six days shalt thou labour and do all that thou has to do', it is written in the Old Testament, but not everyone follows the dictum. People tend to pile up all the tasks left undone during the week to be dealt with on Sunday.

The Island of Sark particularly welcomes Sunday, because on that day they are free of visitors from the mainland.

Mrs R.J. Crimp's delightful poem, read by schoolboy Thomas Long, details the multifarious activities that take place on a Sunday, but the essential holiness of the day is never in the slightest doubt.

SUNDAY REST

Sunday is a special day
For those who live in Sark,
Some rest in bed a-sleeping
Others rising with the lark.

Sunday is a quiet day
No trips from other lands,
The faithful make their way to church
And the vicar reads the banns;

The housewife bakes the Sunday roast
And father pulls the weeds,
The neighbours call for gossip
Or doing useful deeds,

Sunday is a rest day
For doing as you please,
The carriage horses crop the grass,
The drivers take their ease.

Love and Friendship

Back in the summer of 1984 I went to Keswick and in the library of the beautiful Mire House I talked to Dame Anna Neagle about films, the theatre and how, by carrying on with her work, she was able to cope with the loss of her husband, Herbert Wilcox. Dame Anna died in June 1986, but she worked almost to the end.

Her choice of reading, 'Loving and Liking' by William Wordsworth, is what we could expect of a superb actress who both loved and was inordinately beloved herself.

LOVING AND LIKING

I would not circumscribe your love:
It may soar with the eagle and brood with the
    dove,
May pierce the earth with the patient mole,
Or track the hedgehog to his hole.
Loving and liking are the solace of life,
Rock the cradle of joy, smooth the deathbed of
    strife.
You love your father and your mother,
Your grown-up and your baby brother;
You love your sister and your friends,
And countless blessings which God sends:
And while these right affections play,
You *live* each moment of your day;
They lead you on to full content,
And likings fresh and innocent,
That store the mind, the memory feed,
And prompt to many a gentle deed:
But *likings* come, and pass away;
'Tis *love* that remains till our latest day:
Our heavenward guide is holy love,
And will be our bliss with saints above.

William Wordsworth (1770-1850)

The Northampton 'Highway' was devoted entirely to the subject of loneliness, something experienced by everybody at some point in their lives. Certainly it had been experienced by a young lady called Kris Hatherley: she had arrived in a new town with a young child, and no friends nearby, but she had managed to cope and told us how. Kris was responsible for one of 'Highway's' shortest readings – only eighteen seconds. While this extract from a book called *The Gift of Friends* was short, it said so much.

THE GIFT OF FRIENDS

See yourself as a person worthy of love, even if no one at the moment seems to be tripping over his feet with a rose in his teeth to tell you so. But recognise that loneliness won't disappear overnight. It may have to be swept out... each day.

Author unknown

In June 1986 Jimmy Grafton, my friend and agent for forty years, died. Together his family, friends and colleagues celebrated Jimmy's life in the Guards' Chapel at Chelsea Barracks. The Chapel Choir sang some beautiful words, written by Howard Arnold Walter, to an equally beautiful tune, the 'Londonderry Air'.

When we were putting together our Christmas Special, we asked the choir to join us and sing this again for you. So, for Jimmy in particular, I include these words.

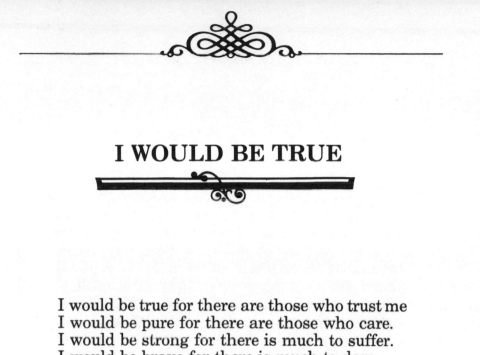

I WOULD BE TRUE

I would be true for there are those who trust me
I would be pure for there are those who care.
I would be strong for there is much to suffer.
I would be brave for there is much to dare.
I would be friend of all, the foe, the friendless.
I would be giving and forget the gift.
I would be humble, for I know my weakness.
I would look up, and laugh, and love, and live.

Howard Arnold Walter

*A*t Great Yarmouth I was delighted to meet up with old friends: Brian Rix and his wife Elspet Gray. They are a couple who do much for the mentally handicapped, so much that Brian has almost totally given up his theatrical work in order to devote himself to MENCAP, the organisation of which he is Secretary-General. In fact, not long after our meeting in Yarmouth, Brian was knighted for his charity work; I can't think of a more popular or more deserved honour.

Elspet provided the reading: a poem from *Answer Me World*, a book which MENCAP had published. I am particularly delighted to include it because this, the title poem of the collection, was specially written for it by Sir John Betjeman.

ANSWER ME WORLD

'Answer me world' is a good name,
It is what we all are saying,
Answer me world with a good game
When the rest of the world is playing.

I'm not made of a different kind,
I don't want to be left behind,
I want to join with the others out there,
Answer me world with your love and care
And let me join in the playing.

John Betjeman (1906-84)

*A*little lesson in statistics. 'Highway' has now exceeded one hundred and fifty programmes, and I have sung at least two songs per programme. Which means – because I am pretty hot stuff at arithmetic – that I have sung over three hundred songs on 'Highway'. Naturally I have repeated quite a few, but it has meant that we have had to cast our net far and wide to find new songs suitable to the sentiments of 'Highway'.

You, the viewers, have been able to help by sending your contributions, and in the course of the search I have been introduced to songs previously unknown to me. Songs which have turned out to be very popular with you. Here is a prime example from our Merthyr Tydfil 'Highway', Joseph Parry wrote the music, Dyved Lewys the words to this song with a message for all of us, which I'm happy to include in this collection.

MAKE NEW FRIENDS, BUT KEEP THE OLD

Make new friends, but keep the old,
Those are silver, these are gold.
New-made friendship like new wine,
Age will mellow and refine.
Friendships that have stood the test
Of time and change are surely best,
Brows may wrinkle, hair grow grey
Friendship never knows decay,
Friendship never knows decay.

Make new friends, but keep the old;
Those are silver, these are gold.
Brows may wrinkle, hair grow grey,
But friendship never knows decay.

Make new friends, but keep the old;
Those are silver, these are gold.
Brows may wrinkle, hair grow grey,
But friendship never knows decay.

For mid old friends tried and true,
Once more we our youth renew;
But old friends alas may die!
And new friends their place supply.
Cherish friendship in your breast,
New is good, but old is best.

Make new friends, but keep the old;
Those are silver, these are gold
Those are silver, these are gold
Make new friends, but keep the old,
Those are silver, these are gold.

Brows may wrinkle, hair grow grey,
But friendship never knows decay.

Dyved Lewys

Walk in Faith

*T*here have been many surveys carried out to find what you, the public, like and dislike about 'Highway'.

One of the questions asked was: 'Do you think that other religions than Christianity should be dealt with on "Highway"?' and we were delighted by the response. Ninety-three per cent of you thought that all religions should be represented.

I mention this because we have found that most major religions have a great deal in common. With this thought in mind, consider the following reading, and if you are not Christian, ask yourself how true it is for your own religion.

It is a particularly interesting passage because it was written by Henry Drummond, a Scottish evangelical writer and lecturer on natural science, who sought to reconcile evangelical Christianity with the new theory of evolution which upset so many, and who therefore needed his religion to fulfil him in both roles.

It was read for us by Alex Monteith in Stirling Castle.

OF CHRISTIANITY

There are versions of Christianity, it is true, which no self-respecting mind can do other than disown: versions so hard, so narrow, so unreal, so super-theological, that practical men and women can find in them neither outlet for their lives nor resting place for their thoughts. With these we have nothing to do. With these Christ had nothing to do – except to oppose them with every word and act of His life. The Kingdom of God, which He proclaimed, is a society, working for the best ends, according to the best methods. Its membership is a multitude whom no man can number; its methods are as various as human nature; its field is the world. It is a commonwealth, yet it honours a king; it is a social brotherhood, but it acknowledges the fatherhood of God. Though not political, it is the incubator of all great laws. It is more human than the state, for it deals with deeper needs; more catholic than the church, for it includes

whom the church rejects. It is a religion, yet it holds the worship of God to be mainly the service of man. This mysterious society owns no wealth but distributes fortunes. It has no minutes, for history keeps them; no members' roll, for no one could make it. Its entry-money is nothing; its subscription, all you have. The society never meets and never adjourns. Its law is one word – loyalty; its gospel one message – love, the greatest thing in the world.

Henry Drummond (1851-97)

I won't forget my visit to York for many reasons. It was very soon after the dreadful fire in the Minster, and I was privileged to meet Peter Gibson who was about to embark on the gargantuan task of replacing all the damaged stained glass. (Would you believe that work is now completed?)

I will also remember York for the following prayer read by Monsignor Michael Buckley.

MAKE US WORTHY

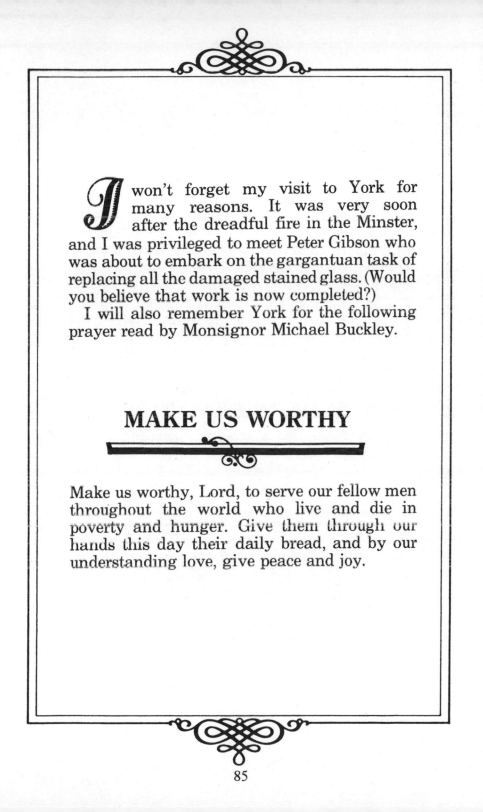

Make us worthy, Lord, to serve our fellow men throughout the world who live and die in poverty and hunger. Give them through our hands this day their daily bread, and by our understanding love, give peace and joy.

In Newry I visited St Colman's Primary School, and was entertained by some delightful children who sang for me and played their own percussion instruments. I think most of us got very excited when one small lad sat with his stick poised over a cymbal waiting for his big moment – when finally it came he tried, not too successfully, to stifle a shy smile of triumph. He was entitled to it for, like the other children there, he was physically handicapped.

The Principal of St Colman's is Brother McQuinlan, and he read to the children – and to us – a poem by Joseph Plunkett which expresses God's existence in everything around us.

I SEE HIS BLOOD UPON
THE ROSE

I see His blood upon the rose
And in the stars the glory of His eyes,
His body gleams amid eternal snows,
His tears fall from the skies.

I see His face in every flower;
The thunder and the singing of the birds
Are but his voice – and carven by his power
Rocks are His written words.

All pathways by His feet are worn,
His strong heart stirs the ever-beating sea,
His crown of thorns is twined with every thorn,
His cross is every tree.

Joseph Mary Plunkett (1887-1916)

*A*t Wimborne in Dorset I chatted with a family of Vietnamese refugees who had found a happy home in that friendly town. Duc Chan told me how he had been living in South Vietnam, studying to be a lawyer, when it was invaded by the North Vietnamese. He was arrested and spent three years in a concentration camp. He later heard of a boat heading for the West but had to leave his wife and one-year-old daughter. Duc spent almost a month at sea before being picked up by a British tanker. I'm pleased to say Duc was later joined by his wife and daughter.

It was wonderful to see a man who had known the horrors of war, false arrest, imprisonment and forced parting from his family, sitting in an English front parlour surrounded by his wife, children and friends. He gave us – in excellent English – a reading that demonstrates the highest ideals of the Buddhist religion.

BETTER THAN A THOUSAND

Better than a thousand useless words is one
single word that gives peace.
Better than a thousand useless verses is one
single verse that gives peace.
Better than a hundred useless poems is one
single poem that gives peace.
Better than a hundred years lived in ignorance
without contemplation is one single day lived
in wisdom and in deep contemplation.
Better than a hundred years lived in idleness,
weakness, is a single day of life lived with
courage and energy.
Better than a hundred years of not seeing the
Path supreme is one single day of life if one
sees the Path supreme.

*J*ohn Wesley, the founder of Methodism, did not believe in making it easy for his congregation. Honeyed words were not for him, nor did he subscribe to meaningless religious clichés. What he did offer was a way of life that emphasised morality and shunned hypocrisy – giving what so many witnesses have been asked to provide: 'the truth, the whole truth and nothing but the truth'.

With this in mind, see if you can honestly face up to this extract from one of his sermons, which was read for us in Bristol by Tony Britton.

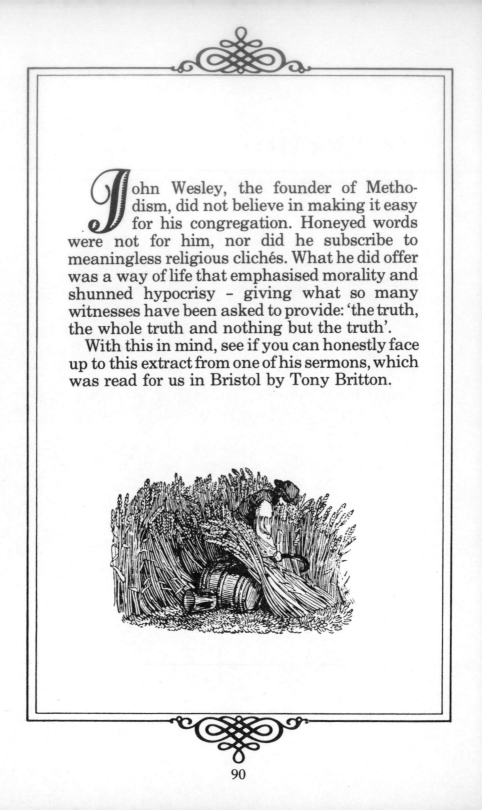

BE DILIGENT...

Be diligent. Never be unemployed. Never be triflingly employed. Never while away time. Be serious. Avoid all lightness, jesting and foolish talking. Converse sparingly and cautiously with women, particularly with young women.

Take no step towards marriage without solemn prayer to God and consulting your brethren.

Believe evil of no one unless fully proved. Speak evil of no one.

Tell everyone what you think wrong in him, lovingly and plainly, and as soon as maybe, else it will fester in your own heart.

Do not play the gentleman. Be ashamed of nothing but sin; no, not of cleaning your own shoes when necessary.

Be punctual.

You have nothing to do but save souls.

John Wesley (1703-91)

The Island of Iona has an unmistakable holiness about it that permeates the atmosphere. It is a place of pilgrimage for thousands of young people who come to enrich themselves spiritually by a visit. Our reading there was provided by 'the Professional himself', Gordon Jackson, and not surprisingly, considering the location, we found the Bible provided the text. If ever you ask yourself the question, 'What does the Lord want of the Earth?', I recommend you read these verses from Isaiah, Chapter 61.

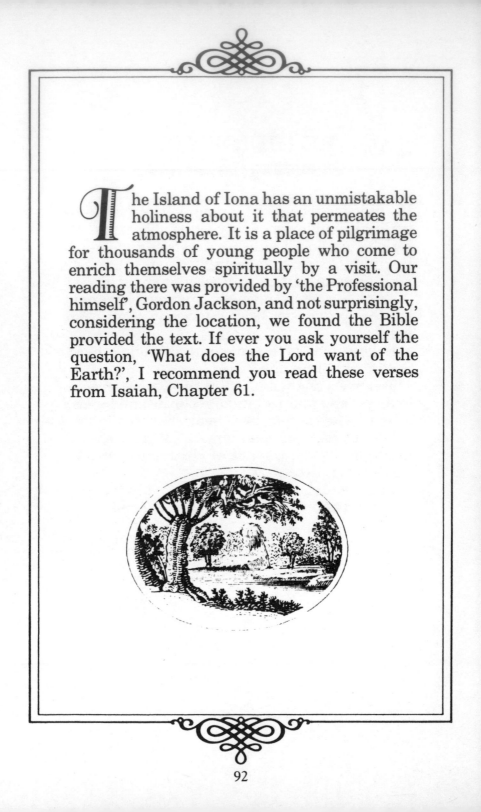

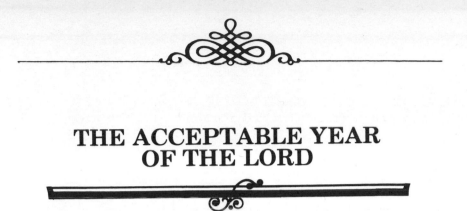

THE ACCEPTABLE YEAR
OF THE LORD

The Spirit of the Lord God is upon me; because the Lord hath anointed me to preach good tidings unto the meek; he hath sent me to bind up the broken-hearted, to proclaim liberty to the captives, and the opening of the prison to them that are bound.

To proclaim the acceptable year of the Lord, and the day of vengeance of our God; to comfort all that mourn.

To appoint unto them that mourn in Zion, to give unto them beauty for ashes, the oil of joy for mourning, the garment of praise for the spirit of heaviness; that they might be called trees of righteousness, the planting of the Lord, that He might be glorified.

And they shall build the old wastes, they shall raise up the former desolations, and they shall

repair the waste cities, the desolations of many generations...

I will greatly rejoice in the Lord, my soul shall be joyful in my God, for he hath clothed me with the garments of salvation, he hath covered me with the robe of righteousness, as a bridegroom decketh himself with ornaments, and as a bride adorneth herself with her jewels.

For as the earth bringeth forth her bud, and as the garden causeth the things that are sown in it to spring forth; so the Lord God will cause righteousness and praise to spring forth before all the nations.

Isaiah, 61: 1-4 and 10-11

J can't leave the Isle of Iona without reminding you of another reading from there. In contrast to the buzz of youth, this was delivered by Lord Macleod, who was nearly ninety at the time:

PRAYER OF THE IONA COMMUNITY

O Christ, the Master Carpenter, who at the last, through wood and nails, purchased our whole salvation. Wield well your tools in the workshop of your world, so that we, who come rough hewn to your bench, may here be fashioned to a truer beauty of your hand. We ask it for your own name sake.

*A*t the risk of repeating myself, I want to talk again about the parallels that exist between so many major religions. But talk is cheap, so let me give you a superb example. It occurred in Luton. Walyat Hussein read an extract from the Koran, and Michael Cann read an extract from the New Testament.

Now, as they say in examination papers – read, compare and contrast.

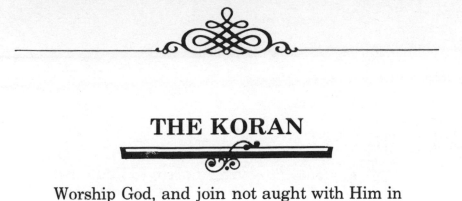

THE KORAN

Worship God, and join not aught with Him in worship. Be good to parents, and to kindred, and to orphans, and to the poor, and to a neighbour, whether kinsman or newcomer, and to a fellow traveller, and to the wayfarer, and to the slaves whom your right hands hold.

THE NEW TESTAMENT

Owe no one anything, except to love one another: for he who loves his neighbour has fulfilled the law. The commandments, 'You shall not commit adultery, You shall not kill, You shall not steal, You shall not covet,' Love does no wrong to a neighbour; therefore love is the fulfilling of the law.

Romans 13: 7-10

On one of my visits to Land's End I met and talked to an artist called John Miller who lives in a former vicarage in the village of Sancreed. Here, a lay Franciscan community has been formed, together with a brotherhood of Christian craftsmen. One regular visitor to Sancreed is the actor Roland Curram, who read for us the words of St Francis of Assisi in the 'Canticle of the Sun'.

The overwhelming humility of the beloved Saint shines through the words.

CANTICLE OF THE SUN

Most high omnipotent good Lord –
To you be ceaseless praise outpoured,
And blessing without measure.
From you alone all creatures came;
No one is worthy you to name

My Lord be praised by Brother Sun,
Who through the skies his course does run
And shines in brilliant splendour;
With brightness he does fill the day,
And signifies your boundless sway.

My Lord be praised by Sister Moon,
And all the stars that with her soon
Will point the glitt'ring heavens.
Let wind and air and cloud and calm,
And weathers all repeat the psalm.

By Sister Water then be blessed
Most humble, useful, precious, chaste;
Be praised by Brother Fire –
Cheerful is he, robust and bright,
And strong to lighten all the night.

My Mother Earth my Lord be praised;
Governed by you, she has upraised
What for our life is needful.
Sustained by you through every hour,
She brings forth fruit and herb and flower.

My Lord be praised by those who prove
In free forgivingness their love,
Nor shrink from tribulation.
Happy, who peaceably endure:
With you, Lord, their reward is sure.

By Death our Sister, praised be,
From whom no man alive can flee.
Woe to the unprepared!
But blest be those who do your will
And follow your Commandments still.

Most high omnipotent good Lord
To you be ceaseless praise outpoured,
And blessing without measure.
Let every creature thankful be
And serve in great humility.

Francis of Assisi (1182-1226)

*A*gain and again in the course of 'Highway' I have been struck by the parallels between major religions. Rabbi Cyril Harris illustrated this when he compared Christmas and Chanukah on our Christmas show. Here's another example. The holiest day in the Jewish Calendar is Yom Kippur, the 'Day of Atonement'. In the services on that day it is pointed out that an evil decree can be averted by three things: repentance, piety and charity, but of all three charity is by far the greatest.

Compare that sentiment to the thirteenth Chapter of St Paul's first Epistle to the Corinthians, which was read for us by the Reverend Bill Morgan from Merthyr Tydfil.

ON CHARITY

Though I speak with the tongues of men and of angels, and have not charity, I am become as sounding brass, or a tinkling cymbal.

And though I have the gift of prophecy, and understand all mysteries, and all knowledge; and though I have all faith, so that I could remove mountains, and have not charity, I am nothing.

And though I bestow all my goods to feed the poor, and though I give my body to be burned, and have not charity, it profiteth me nothing.

Charity suffereth long, and is kind; charity envieth not; charity vaunteth not itself, is not puffed up,

Doth not behave itself unseemly, seeketh not her own, is not easily provoked, thinketh no evil;

Rejoiceth not in iniquity, but rejoiceth in the truth;

Beareth all things, believeth all things, hopeth all things, endureth all things.

Charity never faileth: but whether there be prophecies, they shall fail; whether there be

tongues, they shall cease; whether there be knowledge, it shall vanish away.

For we know in part, and we prophesy in part.

But when that which is perfect is come, then that which is in part shall be done away.

When I was a child, I spake as a child, I understood as a child, I thought as a child: but when I became a man, I put away childish things.

For now we see through a glass, darkly; but then face to face: now I know in part; but then shall I know even as also I am known.

And now abideth faith, hope, charity, these three; but the greatest of these is charity.

1 Corinthians 13

SUMMER—SUNRISE.

The Poet's Voice

Charles Causley is a great favourite with 'Highway' viewers. In our first series we used his poem 'The Ballad of the Bread Man', which was read by Patricia Brake in Bath and was so popular it was included in the first 'Highway' book.

I make no apology for repeating it in this book, and couple with it another beautiful Causley poem, 'I Am The Great Sun', performed by Barbara Jefford at Truro.

I AM THE GREAT SUN

From a Normandy crucifix of 1632

I am the great sun, but you do not see me,
  I am your husband, but you turn away.
I am the captive, but you do not free me,
  I am the captain you will not obey.

I am the truth, but you will not believe me,
  I am the city where you will not stay,
I am your wife, your child, but you will leave me,
  I am that God to whom you will not pray.

I am your counsel, but you do not hear me,
  I am the lover whom you will betray,
I am the victor, but you do not cheer me,
  I am the holy dove whom you will slay.

I am your life, but if you will not name me,
Seal up your soul with tears, and never blame
  me.

Charles Causley (b. 1917)

BALLAD OF THE BREAD MAN

Mary stood in the kitchen
Baking a loaf of bread.
An angel flew in through the window.
We've a job for you, he said.

God in his big gold heaven,
Sitting in his big blue chair,
Wanted a mother for his little son.
Suddenly saw you there.

Mary shook and trembled,
It isn't true what you say.
Don't say that, said the angel.
The baby's on its way.

Joseph was in the workshop
Planing a piece of wood.
The old man's past it, the neighbours said
That girl's been up to no good.

And who was that elegant feller,
They said, in the shiny gear?
The things they said about Gabriel
Were hardly fit to hear.

Mary never answered,
Mary never replied.
She kept the information,
Like the baby, safe inside.

It was election winter.
They went to vote in town.
When Mary found her time had come
The hotels let her down.

The baby was born in an annex
Next to the local pub.
At midnight, a delegation
Turned up from the Farmers' Club.

They talked about an explosion
That cracked a hole in the sky,
Said they'd been sent to the Lamb & Flag
To see God come down from on high.

A few days later a bishop
And a five-star general were seen
With the head of an African country
In a bullet-proof limousine.

We've come, they said, with tokens
For the little boy to choose.
Told the tale about war and peace
In the television news.

After them came the soldiers
With rifle and bomb and gun,
Looking for enemies of the state.
The family had packed and gone.

When they got back to the village
The neighbours said, to a man,
That boy will never be one of us,
Though he does what he blessed well can.

He went round to all the people
A paper crown on his head.
Here is some bread from my father.
Take, eat, he said.

Nobody seemed very hungry.
Nobody seemed to care.
Nobody saw the god in himself
Quietly standing there.

He finished up in the papers.
He came to a very bad end.
He was charged with bringing the living to life.
No man was that prisoner's friend.

There's only one kind of punishment
To fit that kind of crime.
They rigged a trial and shot him dead.
They were only just in time.

They lifted the young man by the leg,
They lifted him by the arm,
They locked him in a cathedral
In case he came to harm.

They stored him safe as water
Under seven rocks.
One Sunday morning he burst out
Like a jack-in-the-box.

Through the town he went walking.
He showed them holes in his head.
Now do you want any loaves? he cried.
Not today, they said.

Charles Causley

What a wonderful poet Sir John Betjeman was. He defied classification, but his work was appreciated by a range of people from the most general of the general public to those they'd think of as 'eggheads'.

Here is one of his poems that can be enjoyed on many levels from the comic to the religious. I am sure Sir John would have approved mightily of the reading of it provided by Patricia Brake in our Marlborough programme.

DIARY OF A CHURCH MOUSE

Here among long-discarded cassocks,
Damp stools, and half-split open hassocks,
Here where the Vicar never looks
I nibble through old service books.
Lean and alone I spend my days
Behind this Church of England baize.
I share my dark forgotten room
With two oil-lamps and half a broom.
The cleaner never bothers me,
So here I eat my frugal tea.
My bread is sawdust mixed with straw;
My jam is polish for the floor.

Christmas and Easter may be feasts
For congregations and for priests,
And so may Whitsun. All the same,
They do not fill my meagre frame.
For me the only feast at all
Is Autumn's Harvest Festival,
When I can satisfy my want
With ears of corn around the font.
I climb the eagle's brazen head
To burrow through a loaf of bread.
I scramble up the pulpit stair
And gnaw the marrows hanging there.

It is enjoyable to taste
These items ere they go to waste,
But how annoying when one finds
That other mice with pagan minds
Come into church my food to share
Who have no proper business there.
Two field mice who have no desire
To be baptised, invade the choir.
A large and most unfriendly rat
Comes in to see what we are at.
He says he thinks there is no God
And yet he comes... it's rather odd.
This year he stole a sheaf of wheat
(It screened our special preacher's seat),

And prosperous mice from fields away
Come in to hear the organ play,
And under cover of its notes
Ate through the altar's sheaf of oats.
A Low Church mouse, who thinks that I
Am too papistical, and High,
Yet somehow doesn't think it wrong
To munch through Harvest Evensong,
While I, who starve the whole year through,
Must share my food with rodents who
Except at this time of the year
Not once inside the church appear.

Within the human world I know
Such goings-on could not be so,
For human beings only do
What their religion tells them to.
They read the Bible every day
And always, night and morning, pray,
And just like me, the good church mouse,
Worship each week in God's own house.

But all the same it's strange to me
How very full the church can be
With people I don't see at all
Except at Harvest Festival.

John Betjeman

The poet C.S. Lewis called himself 'perhaps the most dejected and reluctant convert in history', concerning which I would say I wish that there were more converts like him. His poem 'The Nativity' was read for us by that fine Irish actor Kevin Flood, in Belfast, and illustrates so very clearly the essential humility of the poet. The last verse contains four of my favourite lines.

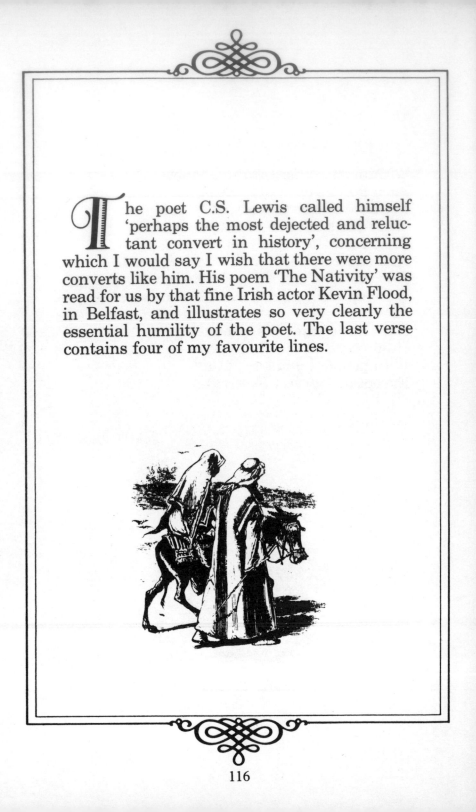

THE NATIVITY

Among the oxen (like an ox I'm slow)
I see a glory in the stable grow
Which, with the ox's dullness might at length
Give me an ox's strength.

Among the asses (stubborn I as they)
I see my Saviour where I looked for hay;
So may my beastlike folly learn at least
The patience of a beast.

Among the sheep (I like a sheep have strayed)
I watch the manger where my Lord is laid;
Oh that my baa-ing nature would win thence
Some woolly innocence!

C.S. Lewis (1898-1963)

I was saddened recently by the loss of a very dear friend, Wynford Vaughan-Thomas, or as he was affectionately known in Wales, Thomas the Talk.

This poem which he read on 'Highway' at St Davids now seems strangely prophetic, especially as its author did not long survive him.

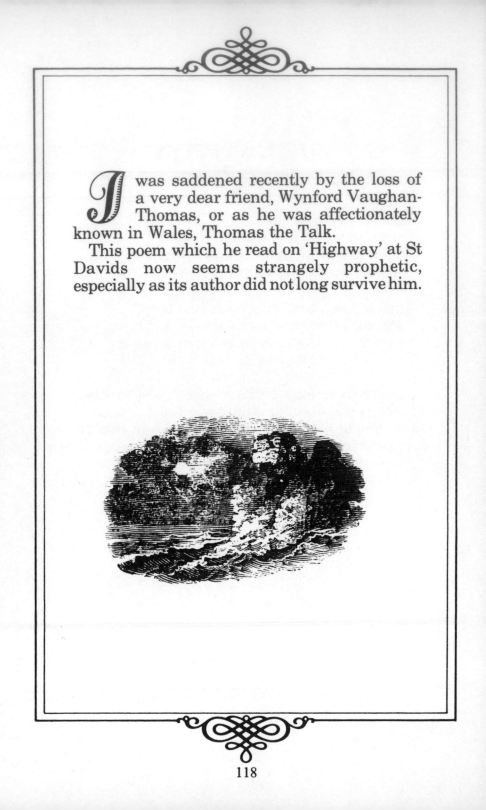

ST GOVAN

St Govan, he built him a cell
By the side of the Pembroke sea,
And there, as the crannied seagulls dwell,
In a tiny, secret citadel
He sighed for eternity.

St Govan, he built him a cell
Between the wild sky and the sea,
Where the sunsets redden the rolling swell
And brooding splendour has thrown her spell
On valley and moorland lea.

St Govan still lies in his cell,
But his soul, long since, is free,
And one may wonder – and who can tell –
If good St Govan likes Heaven as well
As his cell by that sounding sea?

A.G. Prys-Jones (1888-1987)

Say a Little Prayer

What do you want out of life? Everybody must have asked the question some time or another. Here is a pithy, witty, and comprehensive answer. I can't tell you the writer, other than to say it's Anon, but I can tell you that it was read by Dick Graham and came from one of our programmes from East Anglia.

It struck quite a few chords – particularly with one gentleman, who was on the phone at half-past nine on the Monday after transmission. He wanted to have it word-perfect for a speech he was making that day at a business conference. Perhaps none of us, businessmen or not, should ask for more than is asked for in this prayer.

GIVE US, LORD

Give us, Lord, a bit o' sun
A bit o' work and a bit o' fun
Give us all in th' struggle and splutter
Our daily bread and a bit o' butter.
Give us health, our keep to make,
An' a bit to spare for poor folks' sake,
Give us sense, for we are some of us duffers,
An' a heart to feel for all that suffers.

Anonymous

I speak now of Mother Teresa of Calcutta. She may be tiny in stature, but her energy is unquenchable and the force of her example has moved millions. She works among the poorest and the most deprived and her work is never ending.

Mother Teresa's 'Prayer of Reconciliation', read on our 'Highway' from Wavendon, is just what you would expect of the woman. It is as heartfelt as it is simple, and it points the way forward if we have the courage to take that path.

A PRAYER FOR RECONCILIATION

O God the Father of all
you ask every one of us to spread
love where the poor are humiliated
joy where the church is brought low
and reconciliation where people are
    divided
father against son, mother against
    daughter
husband against wife
believers against those who cannot
    believe
Christians against their unloved
    fellow Christians.
You open this way for us,
so that the wounded body of Jesus
    Christ, your church,
may be leaven of communion for the poor
    of the earth
and in the whole human family.

Mother Teresa (b. 1910)

The loss of someone we love is just about the most painful thing most of us are called upon to bear, and when that loved one is only a child the agony is even harder. It's often a period when people's faith is tested to the utmost, a time when comfort is sorely needed and – even more than comfort – an answer to the question we cannot help asking: 'Why?'

This reading from Gloucester Cathedral was given by the Reverend Bob Naylor and an overwhelming number of viewers found these words not only brought them comfort but did indeed help to answer their question. (Gatherers of statistics may be interested to know this reading was a close second to Bernard Cribbins's reading of Canon Scott Holland's message.)

HE WAS SO YOUNG

He was so young, God.

So young and strong and filled with promise. So vital, so radiant, giving so much joy wherever he went.

He was so brilliant. On this one boy you lavished so many talents that could have enriched your world. He had already received so many honours, and there were so many honours to come.

Why, then? In our agony we ask. Why him? Why not someone less gifted? Someone less good? Some rioter, thief, brute?

Yet we know, even as we demand what seems to us a rational answer, that we are only intensifying our grief. Plunging deeper into the blind and witless place where all hope is gone. A dark lost place where our own gifts will be blunted and ruin replace the goodness he brought and wished for us.

Instead, let us thank you for the marvel that this boy was. That we can say goodbye to him

without shame or regret, rejoicing in the blessed years he was given to us. Knowing that his bright young life, his many gifts, have not truly been stilled or wasted, only lifted to a higher level where the rest of us can't follow yet.

Separation? Yes. Loss? Never.

For his spirit will be with us always. And when we meet him again we will be even more proud.

Thank you for this answer, God.

Marjorie Holmes

I take a particular pride in St Patrick – because he's Welsh. But of course I take my inspiration from his words. Here is St Patrick's own pledge to his God, which was read in Belfast by Kevin Flood.

ST PATRICK'S BREASTPLATE

I bind unto myself today
The power of God to hold and lead,
His eye to watch, his might to stay,
His ear to hearken to my need.
The wisdom of my God to teach,
His hand to guide, his shield to ward
The word of God to give me speech,
His heavenly host to be my guard.

Probably the gentlest and most humble of all the Saints was Francis of Assisi. This next prayer, which was read for us by a Franciscan nun, Sister Gemma, on one of our programmes from Glasgow, points us to a way of life to which we might possibly aspire, but which perhaps only a Saint could achieve.

ST FRANCIS OF ASSISI'S PRAYER

Lord make me an instrument of thy peace.
Where there is hatred - let me sow love,
Where there is injury - pardon,
Where there is doubt - faith,
Where there is despair - hope,
Where there is darkness - light,
Where there is sadness - joy.
O divine master, grant that I may not so much
    seek to be consoled as to console
To be understood, as to understand
To be loved as to love, for it is in giving that we
    receive, pardoning that we are pardoned,
    dying that we are born to eternal life.

A prayer need not be any less powerful because it is short. Consider the following one written by Beryl Bye, the author of several children's pony stories which combine a love of animals, adventure and a Christian message.

It was read by ITN newsreader Sue Lloyd-Roberts on our programme from Cheltenham.

PRAYER

Lord, grant that men and women may not be so
concerned with getting that they forget to
give;
That they may not be so concerned with speaking that they forget to listen;
That they may not be so concerned with crowds
that they forget the individual.
That they may not be so concerned with living
that they forget someday they must die;
So that the knowledge that one day we must give
an account of our lives may influence all that
we say and do.

In Your Name we ask it.   *Amen*

Beryl Bye

On one of our visits to Scotland we spent a lot of time in the Glasgow Infirmary. Hospitals are inevitably destined to play a part in our lives, but they are also places where our faith can be strengthened.

I'm sure you have all of you, at one time or another, prayed for a loved one there, but this hospital prayer is a little different. It is a prayer to be prayed by patients themselves, and was read for us by Father Ambrose.

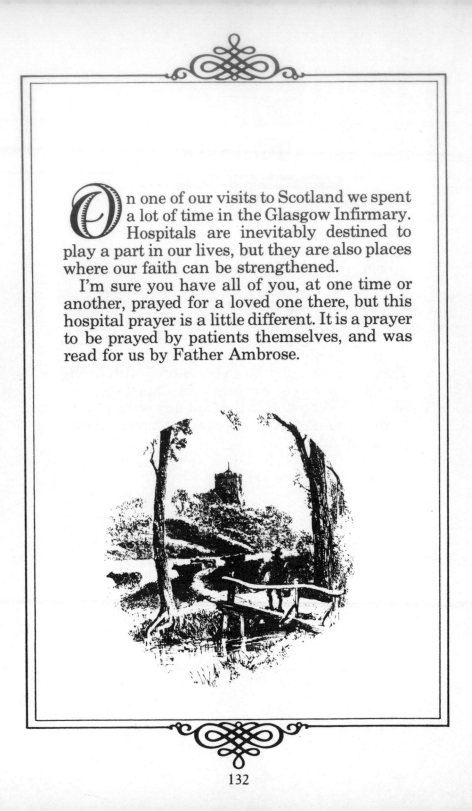

A PATIENT'S PRAYER

Thank you, O God, for all the people who have looked after me today; for all those who visited me today; for all the letters and the get-well cards; for the flowers and gifts friends have sent.

I know that sleep is one of the best medicines for both the body and the mind. Help me to sleep tonight.

Into your strong hands I place all the patients in this ward; the night staff on duty tonight; my loved ones, whose names I now mention; myself, with my fears, my worries and my hopes.

Help me to sleep, thinking of You and Your promises.   *Amen*

Anonymous

*I*n Monmouth, 'Highway' had a pre-Christmas treat when it visited the circus. One of the high spots of the programme was observing the delight in the faces of some blind children as they made friends with some of the circus animals by touch only.

The circus ring was made to look even more enormous as the tiny figure of little Luke Mumford stood there in clown's gear and recited the prayer which is always heard at the Annual Clowns' Service.

PRICES
WITHIN
THE RING.
BY
MERRYMAN.

THE CLOWN'S PRAYER

Dear Lord, I thank you for calling me to share with others your precious gift of laughter.

May I never forget that it is your gift and my privilege.

As your children are rebuked in their self-importance and cheered in their sadness, help me to remember that your foolishness is wiser than men's wisdom.

Traditional

I'm sure most of you are familiar with Tevye the Milkman in *Fiddler on the Roof* who talked to God as man to man. There is an element of that approach in the faith of the Reverend Eli Jenkins, Dylan Thomas's memorable creation in *Under Milk Wood*. Eli Jenkins's prayer is that of a man who will speak to God as he would speak to one of his parishioners.

I still remember the enjoyment I had when I performed it with the Morriston Orpheus Choir in our programme from Swansea.

ELI JENKINS'S PRAYER

Every morning when I wake,
Dear Lord, a little prayer I make,
O please to keep Thy lovely eye
On all poor creatures born to die.

And every evening at sun-down
I ask a blessing on the town,
For whether we last the night or no
I'm sure is always touch-and-go.

We are not wholly bad or good
Who live our lives under Milk Wood,
And Thou, I know, wilt be the first
To see our best side, not our worst.

O let us see another day!
Bless us this night, I pray,
And to the sun we all will bow
And say, good-bye – but just for now!

Dylan Thomas (1914-53)

aying goodbye is not the easiest thing to do. A Cole Porter song puts it thus, 'Everytime we say goodbye – I die a little', but partings have to be faced and they're easier with the beautiful words of this Irish blessing. It's been performed twice on 'Highway': at the beginning of 1986 in Coleraine by the Dominican College Girls Choir, and a little later in the year by the King's Singers in Marlborough. It is a goodbye message that contains my sincerest wishes for all of you.

AN IRISH BLESSING

May the road rise to meet you,
May the wind be always at your back,
May the sun shine warm upon your face,
The rain fall soft upon your fields,
And until we meet again,
May God hold you in the palm of his hand.

Traditional

Epilogue

nd still they come. Just when we thought this book was completed – ready to be 'put to bed' as the publishing term goes – 'Highway' visited Caernarvon. Our reading from the programme produced such an outburst of telephone calls and letters that we had no hesitation in including it as a sort of P.S. I'm not a betting man, but I wouldn't mind wagering that if the wisdom the words disclose so beautifully were acted upon, many so-called 'generation gaps' would shrink rapidly.

The subject is children, and the extract is from a book rich in the philosophy of life, *The Prophet* by Kahlil Gibran. It was read by Elinor Bennett.

I hope you have enjoyed this book. If it helps you on your path through life I will be very happy.

SPEAK TO US OF CHILDREN

And a woman who held a babe against her
  bosom said, Speak to us of Children.
And he said:
Your children are not your children.
They are the sons and daughters of Life's
  longing for itself.
They come through you but not from you,
And though they are with you yet they belong
  not to you.
You may give them your love but not your
  thoughts,
For they have their own thoughts.
You may house their bodies but not their souls,
For their souls dwell in the house of tomorrow,
  which you cannot visit, not even in your
  dreams.
You may strive to be like them, but seek not to
  make them like you.
For life goes not backward nor tarries with
  yesterday.

You are the bows from which your children as
   living arrows are sent forth.
The archer sees the mark upon the path of the
   infinite, and He bends you with His might
   that His arrows may go swift and far.
Let your bending in the Archer's hand be for
   gladness;
For even as He loves the arrow that flies, so He
   loves also the bow that is stable.

Kahlil Gibran (1883-1931)

ACKNOWLEDGEMENTS

If the extracts in this anthology have made you want to read more, the following information may prove helpful. We are grateful to all those who have given permission to include copyright material.

'Walking Away' is taken from *The Gate* by C. Day Lewis, published by Jonathan Cape, and is reproduced by permission of the executors of the author's estate; 'Ruth' comes from *A Rent for Love*, published by the Epworth Press and is reproduced by permission of Mrs Florence Morgan; the extract from the poem 'I like youngsters' is taken from *Prayers of Life* by Michel Quoist, published by Gill and Macmillan; 'Grandfather' is reproduced by the kind permission of its author, as are 'Our Little Fella', 'And Yet', and 'Southampton', which comes from John Arlott's *The Vines*. The extract 'As long as this exists...' comes from *Anne Frank's Diary*, originally published as *The Diary of A Young Girl*, reprinted and published by Vallentine, Mitchell and Co; 'The Final Judgement' comes from the Good News Bible, copyright © American Bible Society 1976, published by the Bible Societies and Collins and is reproduced by permission; a slightly different version of 'I Shall Not Pass This Way Again', can be found in *Songs for Living and Words of Worship* published by the Lindsey Press. 'Something Good Can Emerge' is reproduced by permission of the author. *The Gift of Friends* is published by the Lion Press. 'Answer Me World', by Sir John Betjeman comes from the anthology *Answer Me World* by and about people with a mental handicap, and is reproduced by kind permission of MENCAP; the song 'Make New Friends but Keep the Old' is reproduced by permission of Dyved Lewis and Joseph Parry; 'Of Christianity' comes from *The Greatest Thing in the World* by Henry Drummond; 'Better Than a Thousand' is Dhammapada No.8 from Juan Mascaro's translation of third-century Buddhist writings, published by Penguin Classics as *The Dhammapada*; Charles Causley's poems 'I Am the Great Sun' and 'Ballad of the Bread Man' are reproduced from his *Collected Poems* published by Macmillan; Sir John Betjeman's 'Diary of a Church Mouse' is reproduced from his *Collected Poems* by permission of John Murray (Publishers) Ltd; 'The Nativity' is reproduced from *Poems* by C.S. Lewis by permission of William Collins & Sons & Co. Ltd; Mother Teresa's 'Prayer for Reconciliation' is reprinted by kind permission of A.R. Mowbray & Co. Ltd. from the *Taizé* book; 'He was so Young' comes from *Who Am I Speaking to, God?* by Marjorie Holmes © 1969, reprinted by permission of Doubleday New York; 'Prayer' by Beryl Bye is included by kind permission of the author, and The Reverend Eli Jenkins's Prayer is reproduced from *Under Milk Wood* by Dylan Thomas, published by J.M.Dent. 'Speak to us of Children' is an extract from *The Prophet* by Kahlil Gibran, published by Pan.